Quick & Easy Dinner Solutions

QUICK & EASY DINNER SOLUTIONS

Simple Meal Plans for Your Family throughout the Week

Jenny Warsén

Photos by Ulrika Pousette

Skyhorse Publishing

*A huge thank you to my children who helped
me test all the recipes in this book.*

© Text Jenny Warsén, Photos Ulrika Pousette, 2018
Original title *Middastipset*
First published by Bonnier Fakta, Stockholm, Sweden
Published in the English language by arrangement with Bonnier Rights, Stockholm, Sweden
English translation copyright © 2021 by Skyhorse Publishing

Skyhorse Publishing books may be purchased in bulk at special discounts for sales promotion, corporate gifts, fund-raising, or educational purposes. Special editions can also be created to specifications. For details, contact the Special Sales Department, Skyhorse Publishing, 307 West 36th Street, 11th Floor, New York, NY 10018 or info@skyhorsepublishing.com.

Skyhorse® and Skyhorse Publishing® are registered trademarks of Skyhorse Publishing, Inc.®, a Delaware corporation.

Visit our website at www.skyhorsepublishing.com.

10 9 8 7 6 5 4 3 2 1

Library of Congress Cataloging-in-Publication Data is available on file.

Cover design by Tom Lau
Cover photo by Ulrika Pousette

Print ISBN: 978-1-5107-4627-5
Ebook ISBN: 978-1-5107-4629-9

Printed in China

Welcome

Quick & Easy Dinner Solutions is a collection of simple and tasty recipes to help you out when you just don't know what to cook. A dinner should ideally use few ingredients and serve many. Three words that best summarize my recipes are:

Tasty, simple, and fast!

CONTENTS

Preface

I grew up with my family—my mother Lena and my three sisters Linda, Mona, and Daries—on the Swedish island of Öland. My interest in cooking started when I was in high school, and I mainly enjoyed making the evening meal and batch cooking for the week. I wrote shopping lists for my mother and then either one of my sisters or I would usually have dinner ready when she came home from work. We had a production line going for all sorts of Bolognese sauces, sausage "stroganoff," and casseroles. I rarely followed recipes but enjoyed testing different ingredients and spices. I even enjoyed batch cooking so we could freeze meals for the days we were busy.

When, at eighteen, I became a mother for the first time, my interest in food grew. If nothing else, I had to learn to cook a wider variety of food. This is when I started to write down all my recipes in order to remember the best dishes and how I flavored the sauces. My fourth and youngest child, Nomi, was born in 2009. The same year I started a digital food diary, which is the now the biggest food blog in Scandinavia. I sometimes wonder why it has become so popular. Maybe because it is so simple? I don't want to complicate things, and I choose ingredients that everyone can recognize and recipes with as few steps as possible. Food should be good, but it also needs to be quick to prepare.

Jenny Warsén

Weekly Menus

Weekday meals can be hard to plan, and deciding what to serve up can feel like a bigger challenge than it should—especially when you're juggling a hundred things and out of energy.

This is why I have put together four weekly menus with my, and my family's, favorite dishes. These recipes have saved the day and avoided many potential dinner disasters.

Read more about my menus on page 156.

PORK, BEEF & VEAL

Hearty stews, juicy chops, and grilled souvlaki skewers. Which will be your family's favorite? In this chapter you will find some super easy recipes to help you make a great dinner in no time at all. Stews are also rewarding to make and taste even better the next day.

FANCY PORK TENDERLOIN STEW

Serves 4–6

Food to feed a crowd that takes no time to throw together.

2 pork tenderloins, around 1 pound (500 g) each
Butter for frying
7 ounces (200 g) cream cheese
1 cup (250 ml) whipping cream
2 tablespoons concentrated beef stock or bouillon
2 tablespoons soy sauce
About 1 teaspoon sambal oelek
1 tablespoon roughly crushed pink peppercorns
About 1 teaspoon black currant jelly
Salt and pepper

To garnish
Fresh thyme
Crushed pink peppercorns

To serve
Boiled potatoes or pasta
Boiled asparagus, green beans, or mini carrots

Trim the pork tenderloins and cut them into thin slices. Heat a frying pan or casserole dish with butter and brown the slices on both sides to give them a nice color.

Whisk together cream cheese, cream, stock, soy sauce, sambal oelek, and pink pepper in a saucepan. Bring to a boil and then pour the mixture into the frying pan or casserole dish.

Leave everything to simmer on a low heat for a few minutes or until the meat is cooked through. Add black currant jelly and salt and pepper to taste.

Use pink pepper and thyme to garnish.

Serve with boiled potatoes or pasta and vegetables.

WIENER-SCHNITZEL

Serves 4

A lovely old classic that works well served with green peas and a wedge of lemon.

4 veal cutlets, 3½ ounces (100 g) each
2 eggs
Heaping ¾ cup (200 ml) flour
Heaping ¾ cup (200 ml) breadcrumbs
Butter for frying
Salt and pepper
Chopped parsley to garnish

Peppercorn sauce
1 yellow onion
1 tablespoon butter
2 tablespoons concentrated veal stock
4 tablespoons water
1¾ cups (400 ml) cream
½ teaspoon crushed pink peppercorns
A little bit of cornstarch (optional)
Salt

To serve
Boiled or fried potatoes
Boiled green peas
Lemon wedges

Start with the peppercorn sauce. Finely chop the onion and fry in a saucepan with butter until soft. Add stock, water, cream, and pink peppercorns. Bring to a boil and then simmer for 10 minutes under a lid. If you wish you can thicken it with some cornstarch. Add salt to taste and strain the sauce.

Pound the veal cutlets until they are really thin. Lightly whisk the eggs in a deep dish. Pour the flour into another dish and the breadcrumbs in a third. Turn each schnitzel in the flour, then the egg, and finally in the breadcrumbs. Heat a frying pan with lots of butter and fry the schnitzel until they turn a nice, golden brown color, around 3 minutes on each side. Season to taste with salt and pepper.

Garnish the schnitzels with some parsley and serve with the sauce, boiled or fried potatoes, green peas, and lemon wedges.

HEARTY STEW WITH MINUTE STEAK

Serves 4

An easy dish with lots of flavor. It requires minimal work but needs to simmer for a while.

1¾ pounds (800 g) minute steak
Butter for frying
4 tablespoons tomato puree
1¼ cups (300 ml) water
3 tablespoons concentrated beef stock
2 tablespoons soy sauce
½ cup (100 ml) whipping cream
1¼ cups (300 ml) crème fraiche
Flaked salt
Parsley for garnish

To serve
Boiled potatoes or rice

Cut the beef into half-inch wide strips. Heat a frying pan with butter and brown the meat. Mix in the tomato puree and fry for a few minutes.

Mix in the water and leave to simmer under a lid on a low heat for 1½–2 hours. Most of the water should have evaporated.

Add beef stock, soy sauce, cream, and crème fraiche. Mix it together and leave it to simmer for a few moments, then add flaked salt to taste. Chop some parsley over it and serve with boiled potatoes or rice.

SOUVLAKI SKEWERS WITH TZATZIKI AND MY GREEK SALAD

Serves 4

Lovely oven-grilled skewers, which also work well on the BBQ. The meat tastes even better if left to marinate overnight.

Souvlaki skewers
1⅓ pounds (600 g) pork tenderloin
Skewers

Marinade
½ cup (100 ml) olive oil
Juice from ½ lemon
3 tablespoons chopped, fresh oregano
1 teaspoon dried thyme
1 teaspoon dried rosemary
2 crushed garlic cloves

My Greek Salad
Cucumber
Tomato
Red onion
Arugula
Basil
Green and black olives
Feta cheese, cubed

Tzatziki
½ cucumber
1 teaspoon salt
About 2 cups (500 ml) Turkish yogurt
2 crushed garlic cloves
Some herb salt + black pepper
Olive oil for drizzling

Mix all the ingredients for the marinade in a bowl. Trim the tenderloin and cut into smaller pieces. Mix the meat in the marinade, cover with plastic wrap, and leave in the fridge for at least 4 hours, preferably overnight.

Halve the cucumber for the tzatziki lengthways, remove the inner seed section with a spoon, and roughly grate the cucumber. Pour some salt over it and leave for 10 minutes before squeezing the liquid out of the grated cucumber. Mix the cucumber into the yogurt together with the garlic. Mix and add herb salt and pepper to taste. Drizzle some olive oil over it.

Cut the cucumber for the salad into pieces. Slice the tomatoes and then halve the slices. Thinly shred the red onion. Mix everything together in a bowl with the arugula, basil, and olives and top off with the feta cheese.

Preheat the oven to 375°F (200°C). Thread the meat onto the skewers and grill in the oven for around 15 minutes, turning them now and again.

Serve the skewers with salad and tzatziki.

PORK TENDERLOIN IN A CREAMY GORGONZOLA SAUCE

Serves 4

Gorgonzola adds a great flavor, but if you prefer a milder cheese I suggest a flavored cream cheese for the sauce.

Duchess potatoes (page 53)
2 pork tenderloins, around 1 pound (500 g) each
Butter for frying
Salt and pepper
Finely chopped parsley to garnish

Gorgonzola sauce
1 shallot
2 tablespoons butter
¼–½ cup (50–100 ml) whipping cream
1¾ cups (400 ml) crème fraiche
About 3.5 ounces (100 g) gorgonzola cheese, or preferred flavor
1 tablespoon concentrated meat stock
Salt and pepper

To serve
A crispy, colorful salad

Preheat the oven to 475°F (250°C). Pipe the potato mash along the edges of an ovenproof dish, around 8x12 inches, and broil in the top part of the oven for 5 to 10 minutes, or until it has some color.

Trim the tenderloins and cut them into ½-inch thick slices. Heat a frying pan with some butter and brown the meat for 1 minute on each side, or until cooked through. Add salt and pepper and place the tenderloin slices in the ovenproof dish.

Finely chop the shallot and fry in the same frying pan with the butter. Add the cream and bring to a boil. Remove the shallot by sieving the cream and returning the cream to the pan. Add crème fraiche, crumbled gorgonzola, and stock. Leave to simmer for 5 minutes, stirring occasionally. Season to taste with salt and pepper.

Drizzle the sauce over the pork tenderloin slices and garnish with lots of fresh parsley. Serve immediately with a crispy salad.

SWEET AND SOUR STEW WITH CHILI AND PEPPER

Serves 4

If you prefer chicken you can just swap it, no problem!

1 yellow onion
Canola oil for frying
1 tablespoon tomato puree
1⅓ pounds (600 g) shredded pork (like pork loin)
1¼ cups (300 ml) water
½ cup (100 ml) sweet chili sauce
1 small red pepper, cut into strips
A can of bamboo shoots, around 7 ounces (200 g)
1 ring canned pineapple + 4 tablespoons pineapple juice from the can
1–2 teaspoons white wine vinegar
Salt and pepper
About 1 tablespoon cornstarch (optional)
Fresh cilantro to garnish (optional)

To serve
Jasmine rice

Cut the onion into wedges. Heat a frying pan with some oil and fry the onion until translucent. Fold in the tomato puree and fry for another minute.

Fold in the meat and fry until it has turned a nice color. Add water, chili sauce, pepper, and bamboo shoots. Cut the pineapple ring into bits and mix in together with the juice. Bring to a boil and leave to simmer for a few minutes, or until the meat is cooked through.

Add white wine vinegar, and salt, and pepper to taste. Thicken with cornstarch if you want a thicker consistency. Garnish with cilantro if you like and serve with jasmine rice.

HEAVENLY PORK CHOPS

Serves around 6

Perfect weekday dinner that tends to itself in the oven. Of course, it also tastes good!

6 boneless pork chops
Butter for frying
Salt and pepper
Barbeque seasoning
About ½ pound (250 g) fresh mushrooms

Sauce
1 cup (250 ml) whipping cream
1 cup (250 ml) crème fraiche
1 teaspoon sambal oelek
1 crushed garlic clove
1 tablespoon soy sauce

To serve
Boiled potatoes
Lingonberry jam
Lightly cooked spiralized or shredded carrot
Mache salad (corn salad) to garnish with (optional)

Preheat the oven to 350°F (175°C) and heat a frying pan with some butter. Fry the pork chops on both sides until they have a nice color. Season with some salt, pepper, and BBQ seasoning. Place the pork chops close together in an ovenproof dish.

Cut the mushrooms into quarters and spread evenly over the chops.

Whisk together all the ingredients for the sauce in a saucepan and bring to a boil. Drizzle the sauce over the chops and mushrooms. Leave the chops in the oven for 20 to 25 minutes, or until the meat is cooked through.

Garnish with the mache salad (optional) and serve with boiled potatoes, lingonberry jam, and carrots.

CREOLE STEW WITH CHORIZO

Serves 4

A stew that works both for weekdays and parties with a whole symphony of flavors! If you like you can swap the pork tenderloin for chicken.

1⅓ pounds (600 g) pork tenderloin
Butter for frying
Salt and pepper
2 chorizo sausages
1 large yellow onion
1 red pepper
10 mushrooms
¾–1 cup (200 ml) crème fraiche
1 cup (250 ml) whipping cream
½ cup (100 ml) water
2 tablespoons concentrated meat stock
1 teaspoon soy sauce
Cornstarch (optional)
½ teaspoon dried oregano
½ teaspoon dried thyme
½ cup (100 ml) black olives
½ cup (100 ml) pickled onions
Fresh oregano to garnish (optional)

To serve
Boiled rice

Cut the pork tenderloin into small pieces. Fry the pieces in butter in a casserole dish until cooked through. Season the meat with salt and pepper and remove it and place on a plate.

Cut the sausage, onion, pepper, and mushrooms into smaller pieces. Start by frying the onion for a few minutes and then add the rest. Fry for another minute and then add the meat.

Add crème fraiche, cream, water, stock, and soy sauce. Bring to a boil and then simmer under a lid for around 10 minutes. If you prefer a thicker texture, you can add a teaspoon of cornstarch in a few tablespoons of water.

Mix the oregano and thyme and add salt and pepper to taste if you wish. Mix in the olives and pickled onions and garnish with some fresh oregano (optional).

Serve with cooked rice.

This dish works well for both a weekend dinner as well a larger gathering as it is easy to prepare and you can just double the ingredients.

About 7 ounces (200 g) fresh or frozen
    chanterelles
2 tablespoons butter for frying
2 pork tenderloins, around 1 pound (500 g) each
½ cup (100 ml) water
1 cup (250 ml) cream
1 cup (250 ml) crème fraiche
2–3 tablespoons soy sauce
2 tablespoons concentrated beef or veal stock
Cornstarch (optional)
2 tablespoons lingonberry jam
Salt and pepper

To garnish
A few lingonberries or cranberries
Some fresh thyme

To serve
Oven-baked potato wedges and carrots
Boiled brussels sprouts or broccoli

FOREST STEW

Serves 4 – 6

Divide the mushrooms into pieces. Heat the butter in a frying pan and fry the mushrooms until most of the liquid has evaporated. Remove the mushrooms and set aside.

Trim the pork tenderloins and cut into slices. Then cut each slice into 3 pieces. Place the pieces of meat into the frying pan and fry them until they have turned a nice color and are almost cooked through.

Add water and leave everything to simmer for 5 minutes. Mix in the cream, crème fraiche, soy sauce, and stock and bring to a boil. Leave to simmer for 15 minutes under a lid. If you like you can add cornstarch to thicken it. Mix in the lingonberry jam and add salt and pepper to taste. Add the mushrooms. Garnish with some fresh lingonberries and some thyme and serve with potatoes and carrots, as well as some brussels sprouts or broccoli.

BACON-WRAPPED PORK TENDERLOIN WITH POTATO AND PASRNIP PUREE AND RED WINE SAUCE

Serves 4

An absolutely delicious weekend dinner for the whole family.

2 pork tenderloins, around 1 pound
   (500 g) each
About 10 ounces (280 g) bacon
Butcher's twine, alternatively toothpicks
Butter for frying
Salt and pepper
Fresh thyme to garnish (optional)

Oven-roasted cherry tomatoes
About 14 ounces (400 g) cherry tomatoes
   on the vine
Olive oil
Flaked salt

Potato and parsnip puree
1 pound (500 g) starchy potatoes
1 pound (500 g) parsnips
2 tablespoons butter
1 teaspoon salt
¾–1 cup (200 ml) warmed whipping cream

Red wine sauce
2 shallots
2 tablespoons butter for frying
1 tablespoon tomato puree
1¼ cups (300 ml) red wine
½ cup (100 ml) water
4 tablespoons concentrated chicken stock
½ teaspoon dried thyme
Salt and white pepper
Cornstarch (optional)

To serve
Cooked asparagus

Preheat the oven to 450°F (225°C). Start with the tomatoes. Place the tomatoes in an ovenproof dish with parchment paper. Prick each tomato with a fork or toothpick. Drizzle some olive oil over them and sprinkle some flaked salt. Place the dish in the lower part of the oven and roast the tomatoes for around 15 minutes.

Trim the pork tenderloins and cut into roughly 1-inch thick slices. Wrap a bacon slice around each tenderloin slice and secure with a toothpick or tie it with some butcher's twine. Heat a frying pan with some butter and brown the tenderloin slices for around 2 minutes on each side. Season with salt and pepper. Make sure you fry around the sides so that the bacon gets some color. The meat is ready when it has an inside temperature of 160°F (70°C).

Peel the potato and parsnips for the puree. Divide them into smaller pieces and boil in some lightly salted water for around 20 minutes or until the potato is soft. Strain the water and leave to steam. Place the root vegetables in a bowl, add butter, and season with salt. Mash the potato with an electric whisk. Add the cream and quickly whisk into a smooth and even puree.

Chop the shallots for the red wine sauce. Heat a saucepan with some butter and fry the shallots until translucent. Mix in the tomato puree and fry for another minute. Add wine, water, stock, thyme, salt, and pepper. Bring to a boil and keep boiling until the liquid has reduced by about half.

Strain the sauce and add some cornstarch if you prefer a thicker consistency.

Garnish the tenderloin with some thyme if you like and serve with the puree, red wine sauce, cherry tomatoes, and asparagus.

CHICKEN

Classic and modern chicken dishes with a kick! I love using spices from around the world to liven up the dinner table. Why not try the chicken kebab with pita bread and a homemade kebab sauce—loved by big and small alike. Another colorful favorite is the Balkan inspired chicken dish with ajvar sauce. If you want to serve up something really tasty you can prepare my homemade chicken nuggets.

SPAGHETTI WITH CHICKEN AND BACON SAUCE

Serves 4

This creamy favorite of ours can be prepared while the pasta cooks.

14 ounces (400 g) spaghetti

Chicken and bacon sauce
5 ounces (140 g) bacon
1 pound (500 g) chicken breasts
Butter for frying
1¾ cups (400 ml) crème fraiche
½ cup (100 ml) whipping cream
2 tablespoons concentrated chicken stock
2 tablespoons chili sauce
Salt and pepper
Fresh parsley to garnish

To serve
A crispy salad

Cook the spaghetti according the instructions on the packaging.

Cut the bacon into pieces and fry in a frying pan until crispy. Drain on paper towels to absorb the fat.

Cut the chicken into thin strips and fry in butter until cooked through. Lower the heat and add crème fraiche, cream, stock, and chili sauce. Bring to a boil and then simmer for a few minutes. Season to taste with salt and pepper and add some parsley on top if you like.

Serve immediately with the spaghetti and a salad.

JENNY'S MANOR HOUSE CHICKEN

Serves 4

This dish is always much appreciated and can be served both as a weekday meal as well as at a dinner party.

1¾ pounds (800 g) chicken breasts
Butter for frying
Salt and pepper
5¼ ounces (150 g) shredded ham
1¾ cups (400 ml) crème fraiche
3 tablespoons finely chopped parsley
1 tablespoon Dijon mustard
½–¾ cup (150 ml) grated Manor house cheese (Herrgårdsost), a semi-hard cow's cheese (or use cheddar)
5 ounces (140 g) bacon
Fresh thyme or tarragon to sprinkle over

To serve
Potato wedges or rice
Green beans or cooked baby carrot

Preheat the oven to 450°F (225°C). Season the chicken breasts with salt and pepper and brown them in some butter in a frying pan. Place the chicken breasts in an ovenproof dish, around 8x12 inches, and sprinkle over the ham.

Mix together crème fraiche, parsley, mustard, and grated cheese and spread evenly over the chicken. Place the dish in the middle of the oven and leave for around 20 minutes or until the chicken has an inside temperature of 160°F (72°C). Meanwhile finely slice and fry the bacon until crispy.

Place the bacon and herbs over the chicken. Serve together with potato wedges or rice and green beans or cooked baby carrots.

OVEN-BAKED ITALIAN CHICKEN

Serves 4

A colorful and incredibly tasty meal that can just be left to cook in the oven.

Salt and pepper
1½ pounds (700 g) chicken breasts
Butter for frying
7 ounces (200 g) cream cheese, any flavor
About 4½ ounces (125 g) mozzarella
About 3½ ounces (100 g) sun-dried tomatoes in oil

To garnish
1 bunch of basil
Roasted pine nuts

To serve
Pasta
A crispy salad (optional)

Preheat the oven to 450°F (225°C). Cook the pasta al dente. Cut each chicken breast into 3 pieces, lengthwise. Add salt and pepper. Heat a frying pan with some butter and brown the chicken. Overlap the chicken pieces in rows in an ovenproof dish, around 8x12 inches, and add dollops of cream cheese evenly on top.

Cut the mozzarella into small pieces and cut the tomato into thin shreds. Place everything evenly on top of the dish and bake in the middle of the oven for 15 to 20 minutes, or until the chicken is cooked through or has an inside temperature of 160°F (72°C).

Garnish with lots of basil leaves and roasted pine nuts. Serve with pasta and a crispy salad (optional).

CHICKEN IN AJVAR SAUCE

Serves 4

An attractive and colorful dish that is easy to prepare. The fact that it tastes really good is a bonus.

4 large chicken breasts
Butter for frying
Salt and pepper
1 cup (250 ml) whipping cream
1 cup (250 ml) crème fraiche
3 tablespoons concentrated chicken stock
¼ cup (50 ml) ajvar (red bell pepper sauce)
About 10 cherry tomatoes
½ cup (100 ml) grated mature cheese, like Swiss or Parmesan
Arugula and roasted pine nuts to garnish

To serve
Rice or couscous

Preheat the oven to 425°F (220°C). Cut the chicken breasts into slices. Heat a frying pan with some butter and fry the meat until it is cooked through. Season with salt and pepper. Place the chicken in an ovenproof dish, around 8 x 12 inches.

Whisk together cream, crème fraiche, stock, and ajvar in a saucepan. Bring to a boil and season with salt and pepper. Add the tomatoes. Pour the sauce over the chicken and sprinkle over the grated cheese. Bake in the middle of the oven for 15 minutes, or until the gratin has turned a nice color.

Sprinkle some arugula and pine nuts on top and serve together with rice or couscous.

CHICKEN KEBAB WITH PITA BREAD

Serves 4 – 5

The great thing about this kebab seasoning is that it lasts for several meals—just make sure to keep it in an airtight container. Then next time you make chicken kebab it will be even quicker!

Chicken kebab
2¼ pounds (1 kg) chicken breasts, preferably frozen and partially defrosted
¼ cup (50 ml) canola oil + 1 tablespoon freshly squeezed lemon juice

Kebab seasoning
2 tablespoons cumin
1 tablespoon garlic powder
3 tablespoons chili powder
1 tablespoon ground paprika
2 teaspoons dried oregano
3 teaspoons dried thyme
1 teaspoon cayenne pepper
1 teaspoon black pepper
1 pinch cinnamon

The best kebab sauce
¾ cup (200 ml) sour cream
½ cup (100 ml) crème fraiche
3 tablespoons mayonnaise
½ cup (50 ml) orange juice (strong)
½ teaspoon chili sauce
1 crushed garlic clove
Salt and pepper
Cayenne pepper to taste
1 teaspoon sambal oelek (optional)

To serve
Shredded iceberg lettuce
Diced or spiralized cucumber
Thinly sliced red onion
Cherry tomatoes, halved
Pita bread or mashed potatoes

Stir together all the spices for the kebab seasoning. Keep the mixture in a jar with an airtight lid.

Slice the chicken thinly. Mix in a bowl with the oil and lemon juice. Stir in about 4 tablespoons kebab spice. Leave in the fridge to marinate overnight.

For the kebab sauce, simply combine all the ingredients and set to chill in the fridge.

Heat the oil and then fry the chicken in batches. The meat doesn't need long in the pan, but make sure it is cooked through. Remove to a plate lined with paper towels to drain, and sprinkle with salt to taste.

Serve the chicken with pita bread or mashed potatoes, sauce, iceberg lettuce, cucumber, red onion, and tomatoes.

CHICKEN GRATIN WITH SMOKED HAM

Serves 4

The combined tastes of chicken and smoked ham made this a firm family favorite in our house!

14 ounces (400 g) pasta, like penne or fusilli
3½ ounces (100 g) smoked ham
1⅓ pounds (600 g) chicken breast
Butter for frying
Salt and pepper
Grated cheese for topping, e.g. mozzarella

Cheese sauce
About 1 ounce butter (25 g)
2½ tablespoons flour
1 cup (250 ml) whipping cream
1 cup (250 ml) milk
1 cup (250 ml) finely grated cheese
1 tablespoon chili sauce

To garnish
Fresh basil

To serve
Spiralized or shredded carrot
Arugula
Cherry tomatoes

Preheat the oven to 440°F (225°C). Boil the pasta al dente and discard the water. Place the pasta in an ovenproof dish, around 8x12 inches in size.

Cut the ham and chicken breasts into thin slices and heat a frying pan with some butter. Brown the chicken until it is nearly cooked through. Add salt and pepper. Place the chicken evenly over the pasta and sprinkle the ham on top.

Melt the butter for the cheese sauce in a saucepan and whisk the flour into it. Add the cream a little at a time, whisking the whole time to remove lumps. Add the rest of the cream and the milk while whisking and bring to a boil, whisking all the while.

Add cheese and the chili sauce and stir it until the cheese has melted. Drizzle the sauce over the pasta and top off with some more grated cheese.

Place in the middle of the oven for 10 to 15 minutes.
Garnish with fresh basil.
Serve with carrot, arugula, and tomatoes.

HOMEMADE CHICKEN NUGGETS WITH BASIL SAUCE

Serves 6

These nuggets are another favorite in our house, loved by big and small alike! If you don't want to deep-fry them you can just fry them in a frying pan instead.

Chicken nuggets
2¼ pounds (1 kg) boneless chicken breasts or tenderloins
1 egg
¾ cup (200 ml) breadcrumbs
About 1¾ ounces (50 g) sesame seeds
Some flaked salt
4¼–6½ cups (1–1.5 l) canola oil to fry with

Potato wedges
About 2¼ pounds (1 kg) firm potatoes
¼ cup (50 ml) canola oil
Mixed herb seasoning
Flaked salt

Basil sauce
1 bunch fresh basil, leaves only
1 cup (250 ml) crème fraiche
3 tablespoons olive oil
½ teaspoon mixed herb seasoning
Flaked salt

To serve
Mixed salad (optional)
Lemon wedges (optional)

Preheat the oven to 440°F (225°C). Start with the potatoes. Peel and cut into wedges. Place in a roasting pan and drizzle over some oil. Add herbs and mix so that the oil and herbs are evenly distributed over the potatoes. Roast for around 40 to 50 minutes, or until the potatoes are soft and have turned a nice color.

Using a food processor, combine all the ingredients for the basil sauce until smooth. Chill until ready to serve.

Cut the chicken into 1- to 1½-inch-thick pieces. Whisk an egg in a deep dish. Mix breadcrumbs, sesame seeds, and salt in another deep dish. Turn each chicken piece first in the egg and then in the breadcrumb mixture.

Heat the oil to 345°F (175°C) in a saucepan with high sides. If you don't have a thermometer you can place a small piece of white bread in the oil. If it turns golden brown in a few seconds, the oil is ready to use.

Place the chicken pieces in the oil, divided into 3 batches, and fry until cooked through with a nice golden color.

Serve immediately with the potato wedges, basil sauce, and salad and lemon wedges if you like.

CHICKEN IN GREEN PEPPERCORN SAUCE WITH DUCHESS POTATOES

Serves 4

Duchess potatoes are easy to make and are a fancy alternative to a classic potato gratin.

About 12 chicken breast tenderloins
Salt and pepper
Butter for frying

Duchess potatoes
2¼ pounds (1 kg) starchy potatoes
½ cup (100 ml) whipping cream
2 egg yolks
Salt and pepper

Green peppercorn sauce
The jus from the chicken
½ cup (100 ml) crème fraiche
1 cup (250 ml) whipping cream
½ tablespoon soy sauce
2 tablespoons concentrated chicken stock
1 tablespoon finely crushed green peppercorns
1 teaspoon red currant jelly
Salt

To serve
A green salad

Preheat the oven to 480°F (250°C). Start with the duchess potatoes. Peel the potatoes and boil until soft. Place the potatoes in a bowl and use a potato masher until the potato is completely mashed. Add cream and egg yolks and mix. Season with salt and pepper to taste.

Pipe the mash into small, neat mounds on a baking pan with parchment paper. Bake in the oven for around 15 minutes or until they turn a nice color.

Season the chicken with salt and pepper. Heat a frying pan with butter to a high heat and brown the chicken pieces on both sides until they've turned a nice color. Reduce the heat to medium and fry for 5 to 7 minutes on each side, or until cooked through, or have an inner temperature of 160°F (72°C).

Whisk a dash of water into the frying pan and sieve the jus from the pan into a saucepan. Add the rest of the ingredients for the sauce in the saucepan and whisk together. Bring to a boil and simmer on a low heat for a few minutes.

Serve immediately together with the chicken, duchess potatoes, and a green salad.

Chicken skewers are always a great success in our house, and the kids love dipping the chicken into the creamy peanut butter sauce.

1 pound (500 g) chicken breasts, sliced into strips or cubed
Butter for frying
Salt and chili flakes

Peanut butter sauce
1 tablespoon butter
1 finely chopped garlic clove
1 finely chopped shallot
½ cup (100 ml) finely chopped salted peanuts
½–¾ cup (150 ml) peanut butter
½ red chili, finely chopped
1 cup (250 ml) coconut milk or normal whipping cream
1 tablespoon concentrated chicken stock
Juice of 1 lime
About 1 teaspoon granulated sugar
Water (optional)
Chopped peanuts to garnish

To serve
Boiled rice
Spiralized vegetables
Fresh cilantro to garnish (optional)

CHICKEN SKEWERS WITH RICE AND PEANUT BUTTER SAUCE

Serves 4

Preheat the oven to 350°F (180°C).

Heat a frying pan with butter and brown the chicken on both sides, giving them a nice color. Add some salt and chili flakes. Put the chicken on skewers and place them in an ovenproof dish. Bake in the middle of the oven, turning the skewers every so often, for around 20 minutes, or until they have an inner temperature of 160°F (72°C).

Meanwhile make the sauce. Heat a saucepan with some butter and add garlic and shallot. Leave to fry for a few minutes. Then fold in peanuts, peanut butter, chili, coconut milk, and stock. Bring to a boil while stirring. Add lime juice and sugar to taste. Add water if you want to change the consistency of the sauce.

Pour the sauce in a bowl and garnish with peanuts. Serve immediately with the chicken, rice, and spiralized vegetables. Garnish with some cilantro if you like.

FLYING JACOB

Serves 4

A classic dish from the 1980s that never goes out of fashion.

4 chicken breasts
Butter for frying
1¼ cups (300 ml) whipping cream
1½ tablespoons chili sauce
1 teaspoon yellow curry powder
Salt and pepper
2 ripe bananas
About 10 ounces (280 g) bacon
About 7 ounces (200 g) salted peanuts
Arugula to garnish (optional)

To serve
Boiled rice

Preheat the oven to 440°F (225°C). Cut the chicken breasts into strips. Heat a frying pan with butter and brown the chicken until they have some color (they don't need to be cooked through at this point). Place the chicken in an ovenproof dish, around 8 x 12 inches.

Whip the cream until it forms peaks and then add the chili sauce, curry, salt, and pepper.

Slice the bananas and divide the slices over the chicken. Spread the cream mixture on top. Bake in the oven for 15 to 20 minutes or until it has a nice color.

Finely slice and fry the bacon until crunchy. Add to the dish together with the peanuts. Garnish with arugula if you like before serving. Serve with boiled rice.

SAUSAGE & GROUND MEATS

These are weekday favorites that are quick to prepare. I usually make a beef or sausage dish at least once a week because it's the kids' favorite foods. Try to make a meatloaf, a halloumi baked falu sausage, or why not meatballs filled with cheese? If you plan to try something new from this chapter, I highly recommend the lasagna. It's weekday food at its best, as simple as that.

HEARTY PORK & BEEF SOUP

Serves 4–6

A soup to everyone's taste!

1 yellow onion
1 garlic clove
Butter for frying
1¾ pounds (800 g) mixed ground beef and pork
3 tablespoons tomato puree
4¼ cups (1 l) water
2 beef stock cubes
2 tablespoons soy sauce
1¾ pounds (800 g) canned crushed tomatoes
1½ tablespoons paprika
Salt and pepper
7–8 small, firm potatoes
½–1 tablespoon sambal oelek (optional)

To garnish
Crème fraiche
Fresh oregano

To serve
Rustic bread

Finely chop the onion and garlic. Heat a saucepan with butter and fry together for a few minutes. Push to one side and add the meat. Add a bit more butter if needed, and crumble the meat while cooking, until it is cooked through. Add the tomato puree and fry for 1 minute.

Add water, stock, soy sauce, crushed tomatoes, ground paprika, salt, and pepper. Bring to a boil. Peel and finely dice the potatoes. Mix these into the soup and leave to simmer for 15 minutes, under a lid. Add more herbs (and sambal oelek if you want more heat) to taste.

Pour the soup into bowls, add a dollop of crème fraiche on top, and finish off with some fresh oregano.

Serve the soup together with the bread.

BEEF PATTIES WITH FETA AND CREAM SAUCE

Serves 4

Juicy and flavorful patties with a lovely cream sauce. This is simple food at its best!

Beef patties
1⅓ pounds (600 g) ground beef or mixed ground pork and beef
1 crushed garlic clove
1 egg
1 teaspoon dried oregano
3½ ounces (100 g) crumbled feta cheese
½ teaspoon salt
1 pinch pepper
Butter for frying

Cream sauce
The jus from the patties
½ cup (100 ml) water
¾ cup (200 ml) crème fraiche
1 cup (250 ml) whipping cream
3 tablespoons concentrated beef stock
1½ tablespoons soy sauce
1 teaspoon lingonberry jam
Salt and pepper

To serve
Mashed potatoes (see page 82)
Boiled peas and broccoli

Mix together all the ingredients for the patties in a bowl and work it into a smooth consistency. Shape large patties from the mix. Heat a frying pan with lots of butter and fry the patties until they are cooked through. Place them in a dish with high edges.

Make the cream sauce. Add some water to the pan and whisk into the jus. If you like you can sieve the liquid and pour it back into a clean frying pan. Mix in the crème fraiche and cream and bring to a boil. Add the rest of the ingredients. Season to taste with salt and pepper.

Drizzle the cream sauce over the patties and serve together with mashed potatoes and vegetables.

LOADED MEATLOAF

Serves 4

A juicy, filled meatloaf with cream sauce and oven-baked root vegetables. A word of warning: This will fly off the plates!

Meatloaf
1¾ pounds (800 g) ground beef
2 tablespoons concentrated beef stock
Salt and pepper
5 ounces (140 g) bacon
Some fresh thyme for garnishing

Filling
5⅓ ounces (150 g) natural or flavored cream cheese
5 ounces (140 g) crispy bacon

Cream sauce
¾ cup (200 ml) whipping cream
¾ cup (200 ml) crème fraiche
2 tablespoons concentrated beef stock
1 tablespoon soy sauce
1 teaspoon red currant jelly
Salt and white pepper
Jus from the meatloaf (optional)

To serve
Oven-roasted root vegetables

Preheat the oven to 390°F (200°C). Mix the beef, stock, salt, and pepper in a bowl and make a smooth mixture. Line the inside of a loaf pan (around 2.6 pints/1½ liters in volume) with bacon and evenly distribute the mixture in the pan. Make a large well in the mixture.

Mix the filling in a bowl and place into the well in the meat mixture. Cover the filling with the meat mixture and bacon ends. Turn the loaf onto an ovenproof dish. Bake in the lower part of the oven for 40 to 50 minutes, or until the inner temperature of the loaf reaches 160°F (70°C). Meanwhile make the cream sauce.

Mix cream and crème fraiche in a saucepan. Bring to a boil and add stock and soy sauce. Simmer for a few minutes and then whisk in the jelly. Season to taste with salt and pepper. If you like you can sieve some of the jus from the dish with the meatloaf into it.

Garnish the meatloaf with the thyme and serve together with the oven-roasted vegetables and sauce.

HALLOUMI BAKED FALU SAUSAGE

Serves 4

Once you tire of the usual oven-baked falu sausage, you can try this version to jazz it up! If you can't find falu sausage where you live, use the closest version of a smoked pork and beef sausage.

1 falu sausage ring (or ring bologna), around
  1¾ pounds (800 g)
Dijon mustard
¼ cup (50 ml) relish
½ yellow onion, finely chopped
2 red apples
10 cherry tomatoes
¾ cup (200 ml) whipping cream
½ cup (150 ml) crème fraiche
2 tablespoons chili sauce
Salt and pepper
3½ ounces (100 g) grated halloumi cheese
Lots of chopped parsley to garnish

To serve
Mashed potatoes (see page 82)
Cooked broccoli and cauliflower

Preheat the oven to 440°F (225°C). Score the sausage and place in an ovenproof dish. Brush some mustard in each score.

Mix the relish and onion. Cut the apples into 4 bits, remove the core, and cut the bits into thin slices. Place the relish mix and apple slices in the scores.

Divide the tomatoes and place them in the middle. Whisk the cream, crème fraiche, chili sauce, salt, and pepper. Pour the mixture into the dish and sprinkle the grated cheese over the sausage. Place in the oven for around 20 minutes or until the sausage has turned a nice color.

Garnish with parsley and serve with mashed potatoes, cooked broccoli, and cauliflower.

10–12 fresh lasagna sheets
1⅓ pounds (600 g) mixed ground meat (beef and pork)
Butter for frying
1 yellow onion, grated
2 crushed garlic cloves
14 ounces (400 g) canned crushed tomatoes or passata
¼ cup (50 ml) chili sauce
Salt and pepper
Olive oil for the pan
1¼ cups (300 ml) grated mozzarella
Fresh oregano to garnish

Béchamel sauce
7 tablespoons (100 g) butter
½ cup (100 ml) flour
1¾ cup (400 ml) whole milk
2 cups (500 ml) whipping cream
Fresh nutmeg, finely grated
Salt and pepper

To serve
A crispy salad

LASAGNA DE LUXE

Serves 4–5

A creamy and flavorful lasagna. My secret is adding extra cheese to each layer. I promise it will be a great success!

Preheat the oven to 390°F (200°C). Heat a frying pan with butter and fry the meat, onion, and garlic. Separate the meat well and make sure it is all cooked through.

Mix in the canned tomatoes, chili sauce, salt, and pepper. Let it simmer while you make the béchamel sauce.

Melt the butter in a saucepan. Whisk in the flour and add milk and cream while whisking to ensure there are no lumps. Add the nutmeg, salt, and pepper. Bring to a boil and then simmer for a few minutes.

Drizzle some olive oil in an ovenproof dish. Cover the bottom of the dish with béchamel and then the lasagna noodles. Then layer sauce, meat mixture, grated cheese, and lasagna noodles, about 3 times. Finish with sauce and grated cheese on top.

Cook the lasagna in the oven for around 20 minutes, or until the cheese has turned a nice color.

Serve together with a nice and crispy salad and finish off with some oregano if you like.

MOZZARELLA FILLED MEATBALLS WITH MASHED POTATOES

Serves 4

Cheese-filled meatballs work well for weekdays as well as parties. I usually make the meat mixture a few hours in advance and leave it to stand in the fridge to really give the flavors a chance to develop.

Meatballs
1⅓ pounds (600 g) ground meat (beef and pork)
2 tablespoons concentrated beef stock
1 egg
½ teaspoon salt and 1 pinch pepper
5⅓ ounces (150 g) mozzarella in small cubes
Butter for frying

Pressed cucumber
1 cucumber
1 teaspoon salt
1 pinch white pepper
¼ cup (50 ml) granulated sugar
¼ cup (50 ml) white vinegar
4–5 tablespoons finely chopped fresh dill

Cream sauce
Jus from the meatballs
¾ cup (200 ml) water
¾ cup (200 ml) crème fraiche
½ cup (100 ml) whipping cream
2 tablespoons beef stock
1 tablespoon soy sauce
1 teaspoon red currant jelly
Salt and pepper

To serve
Mashed potatoes (page 82) or boiled potatoes and lingonberry jam if you like

Start with the pressed cucumber. Cut the cucumber into thin slices with a cheese slicer or mandoline and place in a large bowl. Mix together the rest of the ingredients and pour into the bowl. Thoroughly mix together. Place on a plate and put something heavy on top. Leave to chill in the fridge for a few hours so the cucumber can drain properly.

Combine all the ingredients, except the mozzarella, for the meatballs. Make balls from the mixture and make a hole in each ball, placing a cheese cube in each hole and then closing the meat around it.

Heat a frying pan with butter and fry the meatballs in batches.

Mix some water into the frying pan. Sieve the jus into a saucepan and add the crème fraiche, cream, stock, and soy sauce. Whisk to make a smooth sauce and leave to simmer for a few minutes. Mix in the jelly and season to taste with salt and pepper.

Serve the meatballs with the mashed potatoes, cream sauce, pressed cucumber, and lingonberry jam if you like.

SAUSAGE SOUP

Serves 4

The perfect soup for batch cooking and freezing—you just double the recipe! Easy to make and tastes great.

1 yellow onion
2 large carrots
4–5 medium potatoes
1 package smoked pork and beef sausage
Butter for frying
4 tablespoons tomato puree
About 4¼ cups (1 l) water
2 tablespoons concentrated beef stock
½ red pepper
3 tablespoons chili sauce
¾ cup (200 ml) whipping cream
½ teaspoon dried thyme
½ teaspoon dried oregano
Ground paprika to taste
Salt and pepper
Some chopped parsley to garnish

To serve
A lovely rustic bread

Finely chop the onion and slice the carrots. Dice the potatoes and sausage.

Heat the butter in a large saucepan and fry the onion until soft. Mix in the carrots, potato, and sausage and fry for a few minutes. Mix in the tomato puree and fry for another minute.

Add water and stock, mix, and cook for around 20 minutes or until the potato is cooked through. Cut the pepper into small pieces and add at the end.

Mix in chili sauce, cream, thyme, oregano, ground paprika, salt, and pepper. Add some more water if you prefer a thinner consistency.

Garnish the soup with some parsley if you like and serve together with some nice bread.

TACO PIE

Serves 6

Instead of classic Taco Tuesday, make a taco pie. Just as popular every time.

Dough
1¾ cups (400 ml) flour
2 teaspoons baking powder
½ teaspoon salt
3½ tablespoons (50 g) butter at room temperature
½ cup (150 ml) milk

Filling
Butter for frying
1¾ pounds (800 g) ground meat (beef and pork)
2 packets taco seasoning
About 7 ounces (200 g) canned crushed tomatoes

To garnish
1 large tomato
1 cup (250 ml) crème fraiche
¾ cup (200 ml) grated cheese
Fresh parsley (optional)

To serve
A fresh, green salad

Preheat the oven to 440°F (225°C). Mix all the ingredients for the dough in a bowl and knead into a smooth dough. Roll out the dough, place in a springform pan, around 10 inches in diameter, and press it out so that it reaches around 1 inch up the side of the pan.

Heat a frying pan with some butter. Fry the meat for a few minutes while separating and crumbling it with a fork. Add the taco seasoning and crushed tomato. Stir and leave to simmer for a few minutes.

Pour the mixture into the springform pan. Halve the tomato and place evenly over the meat. Mix together the crème fraiche and grated cheese and dollop over the filling.

Bake the pie in the middle of the oven for 20 to 25 minutes or until it has turned a nice color.

Garnish the pie with parsley if you like and serve with a green salad.

FAKE PORK TENDERLOIN

Serves 4

A classic with a twist that really tastes like real pork tenderloin.

1⅓ pounds (600 g) ground meat (beef and pork)
2 tablespoons seasoning mix, or any blend of
  herbs and spices
Butter for frying
Fresh parsley to garnish (optional)

Cream sauce
¾ cup (200 ml) whipping cream
¾ cup (200 ml) crème fraiche
2 tablespoons concentrated beef stock
1 tablespoon soy sauce
Salt and pepper

To serve
Boiled potatoes
Cooked brussels sprouts

Mix the meat and spices thoroughly. Place the mixture on plastic wrap and roll it into the size and shape of a pork tenderloin. Make sure it is completely covered by the wrap and place in the freezer for around 2 hours.

Once frozen, cut the roll into slices. Heat a frying pan with some butter and fry the meat slices until they have a nice color and are cooked through. Place in a dish.

Whisk together all the ingredients for the sauce in the same frying pan. Bring to a boil and then simmer for a few minutes.

Drizzle the sauce over the meat and garnish with some parsley (optional).

FALU SAUSAGE GRATIN

Serves 4

Falu sausage is the best! It's usually a mix of seasoned smoked pork and beef—if you can't find it, just use the closest you can get. This is a favorite of ours and loved by big and small alike.

14 ounces (400 g) pasta (e.g. fusilli)
1 falu sausage (ring bologna), around 1¾ pounds
About ½ pound (250 g) cherry tomatoes
1 cup (250 ml) whipping cream
7 ounces (200 g) cream cheese, any flavor
About ¼ cup (50 ml) mild or hot ajvar (red bell pepper sauce)
Salt and black pepper
3½ ounces (100 g) grated mozzarella

To serve
A fresh, green salad

Preheat the oven to 400°F (200°C). Boil the pasta al dente and leave it to drain in a colander. Pour the pasta in a large ovenproof dish, around 8 x 12 inches.

Cut the sausage into thin slices and spread evenly on the pasta. Cut the tomatoes into wedges and place on top of the sausage.

Whisk together cream, cream cheese, and ajvar. Season with salt and pepper to taste. Drizzle the sauce over the dish and place the grated cheese on top. Cook for 15 minutes.

Serve the gratin together with a green salad.

FISH & SEAFOOD

How about a juicy lemony salmon that can just be left to cook in the oven, or maybe homemade fish sticks? In this chapter you'll find some family favorites with a twist that are both smarter and better tasting than the classic versions. Try to vary classic tacos by swapping the meat for fish or other seafood. It's also a great way to get the kids to eat more fish. Whether you are after something hot, fresh, or tangy, you will definitely find a recipe here.

HOMEMADE FISH STICKS WITH COLD DILL SAUCE

Serves 4

Lots more fun and better tasting when you make your own fish sticks. The sauce will definitely be a hit at the table.

2 eggs
¾ cup (200 ml) flour + 1 teaspoon salt
¾ cup (200 ml) breadcrumbs
14 ounces (400 g) cod, preferably cod loin, frozen and partially defrosted
Butter for frying

Mashed potatoes
2¼ pounds (1 kg) starchy potatoes
1 cup (250 ml) warm milk
A large dab of butter
Salt and white pepper + grated nutmeg (optional)

Cold dill sauce
1¼ cups (300 ml) sour cream
3 tablespoons mayonnaise
3 tablespoons relish
4 tablespoons frozen chopped dill
½ tablespoon freshly squeezed lemon juice
Salt

To serve
Lemon wedges
Boiled green peas

Lightly whisk the eggs in a deep dish. Mix the flour and salt in another dish and pour the breadcrumbs in a third.

Bread the fish: Cut the fish into pieces, turn each piece in flour, then in egg, and finally in the breadcrumbs. Place the breaded fish pieces on a plate. Heat a frying pan with lots of butter. Fry the fish sticks until crispy on both sides.

Peel the potatoes and cut into pieces. Boil in lightly salted water for 10 to 15 minutes. Discard the water. Mash the potatoes using an electric whisk. Mix in the milk and add the butter. Whisk until light and fluffy and add salt, pepper, and some nutmeg if you like, to taste.

Mix together all the ingredients for the dill sauce.

Serve the fish sticks with the sauce, mashed potatoes, lemon wedges, and green peas.

TACOS WITH HOT SHRIMP AND GUACAMOLE

Serves 4

A much-loved fish dish that makes for a slightly fancier taco. Don't forget to chop some cilantro over it—so good!

2¼ pounds (1 kg) large unpeeled shrimp, frozen and thawed or fresh
1 small yellow onion
1 red chili
½ bunch of cilantro
2 tablespoons olive oil
1 tablespoon freshly pressed lemon juice
Flaked salt

Guacamole
2 ripe avocadoes
1 tomato, finely chopped
½ red onion, finely chopped
¼ cup (50 ml) crème fraiche
1–2 garlic cloves
1–2 tablespoons freshly pressed lemon juice
Salt and pepper
Some chili flakes to garnish (optional)

Accompaniments
Tortillas and/or taco shells
Vegetables (any kind), chopped into small cubes
Finely shredded red onion
Sugar snap peas
Jalapeño
Fresh cilantro
Salad leaves

Peel the shrimp and place in a bowl. Finely chop onion, chili, and cilantro and mix into the bowl together with olive oil and some lemon juice. Add flaked salt to taste and some more lemon juice if you like. Let marinate for a bit, then grill the shrimp in a hot pan for just a couple minutes per side, until cooked through.

Mash the avocado flesh for the guacamole with a fork until smooth. Mix in the tomato, red onion, and crème fraiche. Press the garlic into the mix according to preferred taste and add lemon juice, salt, and pepper. Taste and add more lemon juice, salt, and pepper if you like. Garnish with some chili flakes if you want some extra heat.

Serve the hot shrimp and the guacamole with the listed accompaniments.

OVEN-BAKED LEMON SALMON

Serves 4

A fresh salmon dish that can just be left to cook in the oven.

4 frozen and defrosted pieces of salmon
¾ cup (200 ml) crème fraiche
¾ cup (200 ml) whipping cream
Zest of 1 lemon
2–3 tablespoons fresh lemon juice
1 tablespoon concentrated lobster or fish stock
2 tablespoons chopped dill
1 pinch salt
½ cup (100 ml) finely grated mature cheese

To garnish
Shrimp
Chopped dill

To serve
Boiled potatoes, smashed (optional)
Spiralized cucumber
Lemon wedges

Preheat the oven to 425°F (220°C). Place the defrosted salmon in an ovenproof dish. Whisk together crème fraiche, cream, lemon zest and juice, stock, dill, and salt and make a smooth sauce. Pour the sauce over the fish and top off with the grated cheese. Bake in the oven for 20 to 25 minutes, or until the cheese has a nice color and the fish is cooked through, or has a creamy center.

Garnish with shrimp and dill, if desired.

Serve immediately with the boiled potatoes, cucumber, and lemon wedges.

FISH STEW WITH LEMON AIOLI

Serves 4

A simple but luxurious fish soup! To make the best aioli, make sure that all the ingredients are roughly the same temperature.

2 large yellow onions
2 carrots
1 tablespoon olive oil for frying
3 tablespoons tomato puree
4 tablespoons concentrated lobster or fish stock
3½ cups (800 ml) water
6 ounces (170 g) crayfish tails in brine
About ½ pound (250 g) frozen and thawed salmon
About ½ pound (250 g) frozen and thawed white fish (e.g. cod)
15 cherry tomatoes
1 cup (250 ml) whipping cream
1–2 tablespoons sambal oelek
1 bunch chopped dill

Lemon aioli
2 egg yolks
¾ cup (175 ml) canola oil
About 2 teaspoons lemon juice + zest from around ½ lemon
½ teaspoon crushed garlic
½ teaspoon salt

To serve
A good farmer's loaf

Start with the aioli. Place the egg yolks in a bowl and slowly add the canola oil while whisking. Start with a few drops and then move to an even, thin drizzle. Add lemon juice and peel, garlic, and salt. Season to taste with more lemon juice and salt. Cover with plastic wrap and chill until ready to serve.

Finely chop the onion and roughly grate the carrots. Heat a saucepan with oil and fry the onion for a few minutes. Add carrot, tomato puree, stock, and water. Bring to a boil and simmer for 10 minutes.

Drain the crayfish tails in a sieve. Cut the fish into cubes and place in the saucepan together with the tomatoes. Leave to simmer under a lid for a further 8 to 10 minutes or until the fish is cooked through. Carefully stir in the cream, sambal oelek, and dill (saving some for the garnish) and bring to a boil.

Remove the saucepan from the heat and carefully fold in the crayfish tails. Garnish with some dill.

Serve immediately with the aioli and a nice bit of bread.

CAESAR SALAD WITH SHRIMP

Serves 4

This Caesar salad with a twist has shrimp and crispy bacon in it. It's perfect for large groups, and if you are short on time it works just as well to buy ready-made dressing and croutons.

1 pound (500 g) large shrimp, cooked
1 head romaine lettuce
5 ounces (140 g) crispy bacon
Parmesan to garnish

Caesar dressing
2 anchovy fillets
1 egg yolk
1 crushed garlic clove
½–1 tablespoon freshly pressed lemon juice
1 teaspoon Dijon mustard
⅓ cup (100 ml) olive oil
½ cup (150 ml) canola oil
⅓ cup (100 ml) finely grated Parmesan
1 tablespoon whipping cream
Salt, pepper, and a little cayenne pepper (optional)

Croutons
4 slices of bread for toasting
Olive oil for drizzling

Preheat the oven to 390°F (200°C). Start by making the dressing. Chop the anchovy fillets and place in a bowl. Add egg yolk, crushed garlic, lemon juice, and mustard. Mix with a handheld blender and at the same time add the olive oil, pouring it in a thin drizzle. Do this with the canola oil as well. Mix in the Parmesan and cream. Season to taste with the salt and pepper and a smidgen of cayenne pepper if you like.

Place the bread for the croutons in an ovenproof dish. Drizzle over some oil and roast in the oven until they are crispy and golden. Cut into small squares and leave to cool.

Break the salad into bits, rinse, and thoroughly shake off all the water. Spread the salad over a plate and then place the shrimp and bacon on top. Drizzle dressing over the salad and garnish with the croutons. Finish off by grating some fresh Parmesan over everything.

COD TACOS WITH PICKLED RED ONIONS

Serves 4

An exciting way to serve fish. Kids usually love these small tacos and you can put your own stamp on by adding your favorite vegetables.

14 ounces (400 g) frozen and slightly thawed cod
2 eggs
¾ cup (200 ml) flour
¾ cup (200 ml) panko
Butter for frying
Chili flakes for garnishing (optional)

Guacamole
2 ripe avocadoes
1 finely chopped tomato
½ finely chopped red onion
¼ cup (50 ml) crème fraiche
1–2 grated garlic cloves
1–2 tablespoons freshly pressed lemon juice
Salt and pepper

Pickled red onions
See recipe on page 135

Accompaniments
Taco shells or tortillas
Crispy salad
Chopped cilantro
Mango cubes (optional)

Start by making the pickled red onions. Then make the guacamole; mash the avocado flesh smooth in a bowl and mix in the rest of the ingredients. Taste and add more garlic, lemon juice, salt, and pepper if you like. Cover the bowl with plastic wrap and leave it to chill until ready to serve.

Bread the fish: Cut the cod into small cubes. Lightly whisk the eggs in a deep dish. Pour the flour into another dish, and panko in a third. Turn the fish cubes in the flour, then in the egg, and finally in panko. Heat a frying pan with lots of butter and fry the fish cubes until they are crispy and have a nice golden-brown color.

Serve together with the guacamole, pickled red onions, tortillas or taco shells, and accompaniments.

SPICY SALMON WITH COUSCOUS SALAD AND CRAYFISH MIX

Serves 4-5

A fresh and colorful salmon dish. A lot of the heat in the chili is in the seeds and membrane, so remove these if you prefer less heat. The vegetables in the couscous salad can be swapped for anything you might have at home, or ones that you prefer.

1 side of salmon with skin on
Flaked salt
Lemon pepper
Finely chopped red and green chili
1 lemon, thinly sliced
Lots of fresh, chopped dill

Couscous salad
4 portions couscous
½ red pepper, finely chopped
½ red onion, finely chopped
1 bunch arugula, roughly chopped
2 tablespoons olive oil

Crayfish mix
6 ounces (170 g) crayfish tails in brine
⅓ cup (100 ml) sour cream
⅓ cup (100 ml) crème fraiche
About 2¾ ounces (80 g) red caviar
Salt and pepper

Start with the crayfish mix. Drain the crayfish tails in a small sieve and the chop them up. Mix with the rest of the ingredients in a bowl and chill for a few hours before serving.

Preheat the oven to 350°F (180°C). Place the salmon in an ovenproof dish and season with salt and pepper. Sprinkle chili on top and then add the lemon slices. Top off with dill.

Bake the salmon in the oven for 20 to 30 minutes, or until the salmon is cooked through and has a creamy center. Meanwhile make the couscous salad.

Boil 4 portions of couscous according to the packaging (you can make it in vegetable stock if you like). Mix with the rest of the ingredients.

Garnish the salmon with lots of dill and serve together with the couscous salad and crayfish mix.

OUR FAMILY'S FISH BURGERS

Serves 4 – 6

Even children who hate fish usually like these fun burgers. Even better if you serve fries with it.

7 ounces (200 g) fillet of cod or pollock, preferably frozen and partially thawed
7 ounces (200 g) salmon fillet, preferably frozen and partially thawed
1 teaspoon salt
2 tablespoons chopped dill
Some lemon pepper
¼ cup (50 ml) whipping cream (optional)
Panko for breading
Butter for frying

Dressing
¼ cup (50 ml) sour cream
⅓–½ cup (100 ml) mayonnaise
⅓ cup (100 ml) relish
4 tablespoons chopped dill
Salt and pepper

Accompaniments
Hamburger buns
Salad leaves
Tomato slices
Pickled red onions (page 135) (optional)
Avocado slices (optional)

Start with the dressing. Mix all the ingredients in a bowl and set aside.

Cut the fish into small cubes and place in a food mixer. Mix in salt, dill, and some lemon pepper. Cream is optional; if you think the mix is too dry then add some cream. Mix everything together to make a batter.

Shape 4 to 6 burgers. Pour the panko into a dish and turn the burgers in it. Heat a frying pan with butter and fry the burgers for 3 minutes on each side on a medium heat.

Serve the burgers and buns together with dressing and accompaniments.

PASTA WITH CREAMY SALMON SAUCE

Serves 4

A quick and easy idea for dinner—creamy pasta sauce with salmon is always a good choice.

14 ounces pasta (400 g)—for example, fusilli or tortellini
1 yellow onion
About 1 pound (500 g) salmon fillets, preferably frozen and partially thawed
Butter for frying
1¼ cups (300 ml) crème fraiche
⅔ cup (150 ml) whipping cream
1 bunch of finely chopped dill
2 tablespoons concentrated lobster or fish stock
2 tablespoons freshly pressed lemon juice
Salt and lemon pepper

To serve
Cooked and shredded sugar snap peas and pieces of asparagus
Lemon wedges (optional)

Boil the pasta according to the instructions on the packaging. Meanwhile make the salmon sauce: finely chop the onion and cut the salmon into small cubes, around ½ inch x ½ inch.

Heat a large frying pan with some butter and fry the onion until soft. Add the salmon and fry for another few minutes. Add crème fraiche, cream, dill (save some for garnish), stock, lemon juice, and bring to a boil. Season with salt and lemon pepper to taste.

Gently fold the pasta into the sauce and serve together with the sugar snaps, asparagus, and lemon wedges if you like.

A slightly different and fun way to serve cod. The dill potatoes are perfect to serve with it—so, so good!

2 eggs
¾ cup (200 ml) flour
¾ cup (200 ml) panko
1 teaspoon salt and ½ teaspoon lemon pepper
4 fresh or frozen and thawed pieces of cod
Butter for frying

Dill stewed potatoes
1¾ pounds (800 g) firm potatoes
3 tablespoons butter
2 tablespoons flour
1¾ cups (400 ml) whipping cream
1 bunch finely chopped dill
Salt and white pepper

To serve
Lightly cooked carrot sticks
Lemon to squeeze over the fish (optional)

PANKO-FRIED COD WITH DILL STEWED POTATOES

Serves 4

Start by making the potatoes. Peel and cut the potatoes into smaller bits. Boil in salted water until soft. Meanwhile make the fish.

Lightly whisk eggs in a deep dish. Pour the flour in another dish. Mix panko, salt, lemon pepper in a third dish. Turn each piece of cod in flour, then egg, and finally the panko. Heat a frying pan with lots of butter and fry the cod until they have a nice, golden brown color. Meanwhile make the dill stew.

Melt butter in a saucepan. Mix in the flour and whisk to a smooth batter. Pour in the cream in batches and whisk to make a smooth mixture. Leave to simmer for a few minutes. Add dill, salt, and pepper.

When the potato is cooked, discard the water and fold in the stewed dill.

Serve immediately with the breaded and fried cod, the lightly cooked carrot sticks, and lemon wedges if you like. You can use the butter from frying as sauce.

VEGETARIAN

Eating less meat is easy and eco-friendly, and there are lots of good alternatives. Start with one meat-free day a week, you'll quickly see that it's easier and tastier than you might think! There are some great classics here like my crispy potato pancakes, my grandfather's lovely lentil stew, and some dinner favorites in a vegetarian format such as halloumi stroganoff. There are even some hearty stews, some nifty Asian dishes, and other favorites with tons of flavor. Most of the recipes are super easy to batch cook too, perfect for those days when there is simply not enough time to cook!

COLORFUL WOK WITH NOODLES

Serves 4

Feel free to vary the vegetables you use in this dish according to what you and your family like.

2 red onions
1 red pepper
1 green pepper
14 ounces (400 g) spaghetti, soba, ramen, or egg
  noodles
2 tablespoons canola oil for frying
14 ounces (400 g) canned baby corn
⅔ cup (150 ml) raw cashews
¾ cup (200 ml) teriyaki sauce
Fresh cilantro to garnish with

To serve
Lime wedges (optional)

Cut the red onions into thin wedges. Cut the peppers into strips.

Boil the noodles according to the instructions on the packaging. Meanwhile start to prepare the wok. Heat up a wok or large frying pan with oil on a medium heat. Brown the onions, baby corn, and peppers while stirring. They need to get some color while staying crispy. Add the cashew nuts and teriyaki sauce while stirring.

Once cooked, discard the water from the noodles and fold them into the wok. Mix thoroughly.

Garnish with some cilantro and serve immediately; add some lime wedges if you like.

GRANDDAD'S TASTY LENTIL STEW

Serves 4

A lentil stew full of flavor, perfect for freezing if you have any leftovers.

1 cup (250 ml) dried red lentils
1 yellow onion
2 garlic cloves
1 carrot
Butter for frying
1 tablespoon tomato puree
14 ounces (400 g) canned crushed tomatoes
Approximately 3–4 cups water
1 pinch granulated sugar
1 teaspoon sambal oelek
1 tablespoon chili sauce
1 tablespoon red wine vinegar
1 teaspoon salt
Pepper
Chopped parsley for garnish

To serve
Crème fraiche
Cheese sandwiches with a variety of colorful
    peppers

Start by thoroughly rinsing the lentils with cold water in a sieve. Leave to drain.

Peel and finely chop onion and garlic. Finely grate the carrot. Heat a frying pan with butter and fry the vegetables until the onion is soft. Add tomato puree and fry for a further minute.

Add crushed tomatoes, water, sugar, rinsed lentils, sambal oelek, and chili sauce. Bring to a boil and simmer under a lid for about 10 to 15 minutes. Add a bit more water if you want a thinner consistency. Add vinegar, salt, and pepper to taste.

Add a dab of crème fraiche and some parsley to each portion.

Serve together with cheese sandwiches and peppers.

CABBAGE SOUP WITH ROOT VEGETABLES

Serves 4

A lovely vegetarian soup that is full of flavor.

½ small head white cabbage
1 large yellow onion
2 garlic cloves
2 potatoes
2 carrots
Canola oil for frying
2 tablespoons tomato puree
14 ounces (400 g) canned crushed tomatoes
6⅓ cups (1.5 l) water
2 cubes vegetable stock bouillon
½ red pepper
1 tablespoon chopped frozen parsley
½ tablespoon soy sauce
1 teaspoon sambal oelek
Salt and pepper

To serve
Sourdough bread
Crème fraiche

Shred the cabbage. Chop the onion and garlic. Finely dice the potatoes and carrots. Heat a saucepan with some canola oil and fry everything together on a medium heat, stirring occasionally.

Add the tomato puree and fry while stirring for 1 minute. Add crushed tomatoes, water, and stock. Bring to a boil and simmer for 10 to 15 minutes or until the vegetables are soft.

Shred the pepper and mix into the soup—the pepper doesn't need to boil for long as it loses its crispness. Add parsley, soy sauce, and sambal oelek. Add salt and pepper to taste.

Serve the soup with a good sourdough bread and some crème fraiche on the side. Delicious to add a dab of crème fraiche to each bowl!

BROCCOLI AND BLUE CHEESE PIE

Serves 5

A creamy broccoli pie with a touch of blue cheese.

Dough
11 tablespoons (150 g) butter
1½ cups (350 ml) flour
3 tablespoons cold water
½ teaspoon salt

Filling
5 ounces (140 g) blue cheese
1 pound (500 g) broccoli florets
4 eggs
1¾ cups (400 ml) whipping cream
Salt and black pepper
¾–1 cup (200 ml) grated mozzarella cheese
10 cherry tomatoes

To serve
A tasty and colorful salad

Preheat the oven to 390°F (200°C). Start with the dough. Cut the butter into cubes and add to a bowl with the rest of the ingredients. Quickly knead and work into a dough, cover with plastic wrap, and leave it to chill in the fridge for 20 minutes.

Press the dough into a rectangular pan, pressing the dough up along the edges. Prick the base with a fork and blind-bake the pie crust for 10 minutes.

Dice the blue cheese and break the broccoli into florets; place both into the pie crust.

Whisk together eggs and cream and add some salt and pepper (remember, the blue cheese is salty in itself). Drizzle the egg batter over the filling and sprinkle the grated cheese on top. Halve the tomatoes and add on top of the pie. Bake for 20 to 30 minutes, or until the pie has a nice color.

Serve immediately with a salad.

PASTA WITH A CREAMY VEGETABLE SAUCE

Serves 4

The whole family will appreciate this lovely, colorful dish.

14 ounces (400 g) pasta, e.g. farfalle or penne
1 yellow onion
1 garlic clove
2 carrots
1 zucchini
Butter for frying
14 ounces (400 g) canned passata or crushed
  tomatoes
2–4 tablespoons ajvar (preferably hot)
3½ ounces (100 g) fresh baby spinach
1 cup (250 ml) crème fraiche
Salt and black pepper

To garnish
Some fresh oregano
Grated Parmesan

Boil the pasta according to the instructions on the packaging. Meanwhile make the sauce: finely grate the onion and garlic and roughly grate carrots and zucchini.

Heat a frying pan with butter and fry the onion and garlic for 1 minute or so. Add the carrots and zucchini and fry for another couple of minutes. Add passata or crushed tomatoes, ajvar, spinach, and crème fraiche and mix. Add salt and pepper to taste and finish off with some oregano and Parmesan.

Serve immediately together with the pasta and some freshly ground black pepper.

POTATO PANCAKES WITH LINGONBERRIES

Serves 4

Basic, hearty food at its best!

10 firm, large potatoes (at least 1¾ pounds)
1 cup (250 ml) flour
2½ cups (600 ml) whole milk
3 eggs
1 teaspoon salt
Butter for frying

To serve
Lingonberries (or cranberry sauce)
Grated carrot mixed with some fresh flat-leaf
   parsley

Peel and roughly grate the potatoes and place in
a bowl. In another bowl, whisk the flour with a
little bit of milk at a time to make a smooth batter.
Whisk in the eggs and salt.

Pour the batter into the grated potato. Heat a
frying pan with some butter and fry 2 pancakes
at a time for a few minutes on each side until they
are golden brown. If you have another frying pan
you can use that at the same time to speed things
up.

Serve the potato pancakes with some
lingonberries or cranberry sauce, carrot, and
parsley.

HALLOUMI STROGANOFF

Serves 4

A vegetarian dish that the whole family with love!

1 yellow onion
14 ounces (400 g) halloumi
Butter for frying
2 tablespoons tomato puree
¾ cup (200 ml) whipping cream
¾ cup (200 ml) crème fraiche
1 teaspoon soy sauce
½ teaspoon dried thyme
Salt and black pepper

To serve
Boiled rice
An arugula, tomato, red onion, and cucumber
    salad

Finely chop the onion. Cut the halloumi into batons. Heat a frying pan with some butter and fry the cheese on all sides to give it some color. Remove the cheese batons from the frying pan and fry the finely chopped onion until translucent. Add the tomato puree, cream, and crème fraiche and bring to a boil.

Season to taste with soy sauce, thyme, salt, and pepper. Finally add the cheese and make sure everything is heated through.

Serve immediately with rice and salad.

VEGETABLE PATTIES WITH HALLOUMI

Serves 4

These little beauties can be served together with mashed potatoes, or you can make 2 larger patties and serve them in hamburger buns together with various accompaniments. You can also swap the carrots for zucchini.

14 ounces (400 g) halloumi
1 pound (500 g) carrots
4 eggs
¾ cup (200 ml) breadcrumbs
1 teaspoon salt
Chili flakes
4 tablespoons finely chopped parsley
Butter for frying
Some fresh thyme for garnishing (optional)

To serve
Mashed potatoes (page 82)
A nice salad

Roughly grate the halloumi and carrots. Mix everything in a bowl together with the rest of the ingredients. Leave to sit for 5 minutes.

Shape the mix into 8 small patties. Heat a frying pan with butter and fry the patties for 3 to 4 minutes on each side, or until they have a nice color.

Garnish the patties with thyme if you like and serve together with mashed potatoes and salad.

THAI RED STEW

Serves 4

This stew is a favorite on our meat-free days. You just have to try it!

1 yellow onion
1 large sweet potato
Canola oil to fry
1½ tablespoons red curry paste
14 ounces (400 g) canned crushed tomatoes with garlic
⅔ cup (150 ml) water
14 ounces (400 g) canned coconut milk
14 ounces (400 g) canned chickpeas
1½ inches fresh ginger, grated
1 red chili, finely chopped
5–6 ounces (150 g) baby spinach
Juice of 1 lime

To serve
Boiled rice, preferably jasmine

Chop the onion. Peel and cut the sweet potato in ½- x ½ -inch cubes. Heat a deep frying pan with canola oil. Add onion and curry paste and leave to fry while stirring for a few minutes.

Mix in the sweet potato, crushed tomatoes, and water. Bring to a boil, then reduce the heat and leave to simmer under a lid until the sweet potato is soft. Add the coconut milk, chickpeas, ginger, and chili and bring to a boil. Remove the pan from the heat. Add the spinach and lime juice.

Serve together with jasmine rice.

PASTA WITH HOMEMADE PESTO

Serves 4

A lovely green pesto that both smells and tastes heavenly!

14 ounces (400 g) pasta, any kind
Cherry tomatoes, cut in wedges to serve (optional)

Pesto
2 bunches of fresh basil
1¾ ounces (50 g) pine nuts
1 garlic clove
⅔–¾ cup (150–200 ml) olive oil
3½ ounces (100 g) grated Parmesan
2 pinches salt
Freshly ground black pepper

Boil the pasta according to the instructions on the packaging.

Remove the basil leaves from the stalks (put some aside for garnishing). Roast the pine nuts in a dry frying pan and then pulse in a food processor. Roughly chop the garlic and add this and the basil to the food processor. Mix together and add olive oil in a drizzle until you get the right consistency. Finally add the Parmesan. Season with salt and pepper.

Add the pesto to your pasta and garnish with some basil leaves and serve together with cherry tomatoes if you like.

PARTIES & FESTIVITIES

In this chapter you will find easy-to-prepare party food! Lovely recipes that are perfect for weekend dinners with the family as well as at get-togethers. The recipes are great to serve up to friends, such as Langos—a Hungarian dish that tastes great and can be eaten with all sorts of accompaniments. Or what about my family's pizza? You can experiment with the toppings, and it's a great way to get rid of any leftover food at the end of the week.

1¾-pound (800 g) piece of beef sirloin
Butter for frying
Salt and pepper

Luxurious hasselback potatoes
8–12 normal size firm potatoes
Melted butter for brushing
5 ounces (140 g) bacon
Cheese slices such as Gouda, divided into 3
Finely chopped fresh parsley to garnish

Blue cheese sauce
The fat from the fried bacon
½ cup (100 ml) water
½ cup (100 ml) crème fraiche
1 cup (250 ml) whipping cream
½ tablespoon soy sauce
About 5⅓ ounces (150 g) blue cheese
1 teaspoon runny honey
Pepper and salt (optional)

To serve
A green salad

ROAST SIRLOIN OF BEEF WITH LUXURIOUS HASSELBACK POTATOES AND BLUE CHEESE SAUCE

Serves 4

Leave the meat at room temperature for 2 to 3 hours before preparing. As the meat and potatoes are cooked at the same time in the oven, the sirloin can be slightly thinner so that they can cook for the same amount of time.

Preheat the oven to 390°F (200°C). Heat a frying pan with butter and fry the beef on all sides to give it some color. Add salt and pepper. Place the meat in an ovenproof dish and put a thermometer in the thickest part of the meat.

Carefully clean the potatoes and thinly slice them but not all the way through. Place them in an ovenproof dish and brush with melted butter. Place the dish with the meat at the bottom of the oven and the potatoes on top.

Make the sauce and the bacon: Slice the bacon and fry until crispy in a frying pan. Leave to drain on some paper towels. Whisk some water for the sauce into the frying pan and bring to a boil. Add crème fraiche, cream, and soy sauce and mix. Crumble the blue cheese into it and stir until melted. Add honey and pepper to taste and some salt if you like.

Remove the meat when it has an inner temperature of 136.4°F to 140°F (58°C to 60°C, equivalent to medium done) and wrap in aluminum foil. Remove the potatoes after about 45 minutes and place some cheese in each score. Place in the oven until the cheese has melted.

Crumble bacon and parsley over the potato and serve together with slices of beef, sauce, and a salad.

PLANKED SALMON

Makes 4 planks/portions

This is a fun and tasty way to serve salmon. You can find the planks for cooking in a butcher's shop or online. You can also use a regular ovenproof dish.

Duchess potatoes (page 53)
2 tablespoons dried dill
4 fresh pieces of salmon, around 5.3 ounces (150 g) each
Salt and pepper
About ½ pound (250 g) cherry tomatoes

To garnish
Large, good quality cooked, peeled shrimp
A few sprigs of dill
Lemon wedges (optional)
Cooked asparagus, both green and white (optional)

Lemon sauce
1 cup (250 ml) whipping cream
¾ cup (200 ml) crème fraiche
½ tablespoon concentrated lobster or fish stock
2 tablespoons freshly squeezed lemon juice

Preheat the oven to 400°F to 440°F (200°C to 225°C). Start with the duchess potatoes and mix the mash with the dried dill.

Heat the planks in the oven for around 5 minutes. Oil them and then place the salmon on top. Add salt and pepper and bake in the oven for around 15 minutes.

Increase the temperature to 480°F (250°C). Pipe and dab the duchess potatoes on the planks. Halve the tomatoes and place them over the plank and return to the oven for 5 to 10 minutes or until the potatoes have a nice color.

Whisk together all the ingredients for the sauce, except the lemon juice, in a saucepan. Bring to a boil and then remove from the heat. Add the lemon juice to taste.

Garnish the planks with sauce, shrimp, sprigs of dill, and if you like, lemon wedges and asparagus.

LANGOS

*16 small langos
Serves around 4*

Langos is a Hungarian-style deep-fried flatbread popular in Sweden. It makes the perfect weekend dinner with the family. Everyone can help themselves and vary the toppings according to their preference. My favorite is shrimp with red caviar.

Langos dough
0.9 ounce (25 g) yeast
1¼ cups (300 ml) lukewarm water
1 teaspoon salt
1 boiled and mashed potato
About 3 cups (700 ml) flour
4¼ cups (1 l) canola oil for deep frying

Sour cream sauce
½ cup (100 ml) sour cream
½ cup (100 ml) crème fraiche
1 garlic clove, pressed
Salt and pepper

Accompaniments
1 pound (500 g) cooked, peeled shrimp
2 finely chopped red onions
1 can red or black caviar
½–¾ cup (100–200 ml) grated mature cheese

Crumble the yeast into a bowl, add the water, and stir until the yeast has dissolved. Add salt, the mashed potato, and flour and work into a smooth, loose dough. Cover the bowl and leave to rise for around 40 minutes.

Turn the dough out onto a well-floured surface. Divide into 16 portions and roll each one out until it is about ½-inch thick. Use more flour if you need. Place the pieces on floured parchment paper, cover with a baking towel, and leave to rise for 15 minutes.

Mix all the ingredients for the sauce together and leave to chill for 10 minutes before serving.

Pour the oil in a deep fryer or a saucepan with a thick bottom. Heat the oil to around 345°F (175°C). If you don't have a thermometer, you can add a bit of white bread to the oil. If it turns golden brown in a few seconds, the oil is hot enough. Fry a couple pieces of dough at a time until they turn a nice color, around 3 minutes on each side. Leave the bread to drain on some paper towels.

Serve the bread together with the accompaniments and the sauce.

SANDWICH CAKE

Serve around 8

This cake can be prepared the day before, and then you can just decorate it on the day. This makes it moist and tasty!

8 slices of round soft bread (Polarbröd) divided into half-moon shapes (or use pita bread)
10½ ounces (300 g) plain cream cheese

Liver paté filling (2 layers)
14 ounces (400 g) spreadable liver paté
1¼ cups (300 ml) crème fraiche
3½ ounces (100 g) plain cream cheese
4 tablespoons relish

Egg and ham filling (1 layer)
2 finely chopped hard-boiled eggs
3½ ounces (100 g) cream cheese
¾ pound (350 g) chopped smoked ham
1 teaspoon Dijon mustard
About ¾ cup (200 ml) basic mix (see below)

Basic mix to cover the cake with
1¼ cups (300 ml) whipped cream
¾ cup (200 ml) crème fraiche
3 tablespoons mayonnaise

Suggestions for garnish
Ham
Cheese, e.g. Gouda
Chopped red onion
Hard-boiled eggs
Grapes
Cucumber slices
Large, cooked and peeled shrimp
Thinly sliced star fruit
Different types of salad
Sprigs of dill
Fish roe
Lemon slices

Mix together the fillings in different bowls. Spread a thick layer of cream cheese on all the pieces of bread and place 2 of them together to form a circle.

Spread half the liver paté filling on top. Then add to pieces of bread on top of that and spread the egg and ham filling on top. Repeat this process with the rest of the bread and filling.

Lastly, cover the cake with the basic mix. Cover the cake in plastic wrap and leave it in the fridge overnight. Then decorate the cake just before you serve it.

PULLED PORK WITH PICKLED RED ONIONS

Serves 6

If you pickle the onion the night before, it tastes better as the flavors have more time to meld. You can also massage the onion into the liquid—in that case you only need to prepare it an hour or so in advance.

Pulled pork
2⅔ pounds (1.2 kg) pork butt
Oil for greasing
Salt and pepper
2 yellow onions
1 cup (250 ml) barbecue sauce (not too sweet)
1 garlic clove

Pickled red onions
2 large red onions
1¼ cups (300 ml) water
½ cup (100 ml) white vinegar
⅔ cup (150 ml) granulated sugar

Garlic sauce
1 cup (250 ml) crème fraiche
1 crushed garlic clove
2 tablespoons chili sauce
½ teaspoon dried thyme
Salt and pepper

To serve
Hamburger buns, pita bread, or tortillas
Crispy lettuce leaves
Tomato slices
Cilantro leaves

Start with the pickled red onions. Thinly slice the onion and place in a container with a lid. Mix the water, white vinegar, and sugar to make a syrup and bring to a boil. Leave to cool and pour into the container. Add the lid and leave in the fridge until the next day.

Preheat the oven to 215°F to 250°F (100°C to 120°C). Drizzle some oil in the bottom of an ovenproof dish with a lid. Add the meat and season with salt and pepper, rubbing them into the meat. Chop the onions and finely chop the garlic and add to the meat. Evenly distribute barbecue sauce over the meat, add the lid, and place in the lower part of the oven for 4 to 5 hours. You should test the meat after 4 hours—it is ready when you can easily separate it with a fork. If it is not tender enough, leave it for a bit longer. Then pull the whole piece of meat apart with a fork.

Mix the ingredients for the garlic sauce together. Serve the meat together with the sauce, pickled red onions, some nice bread, salad leaves, tomato slices, and cilantro.

THE FISH WIVES' LUXURIOUS FISH STEW

Serves 6

A fancier fish stew with lobster sauce.

4 frozen and thawed pieces of salmon
14 ounces (400 g) frozen and thawed cod fillet
1¾ cups (400 ml) whipping cream
7 ounces (200 g) cream cheese
2 tablespoons concentrated lobster stock
2 tablespoons chopped dill
½ teaspoon curry powder
Salt and pepper
About 8 ounces (250 g) cherry tomatoes (both red and yellow)

To garnish
As many cooked and peeled shrimp as you like

To serve
Rice, pasta, or boiled potatoes
Cooked green asparagus or broccoli

Preheat the oven to 450°F (225°C). Cut the fish into 1 x 1-inch pieces and place in an ovenproof dish.

Whisk together the cream, cream cheese, stock, dill, curry, salt, and pepper in a saucepan. Slowly bring to a boil and then drizzle the sauce over the fish. Sprinkle some cherry tomatoes over it and place in the oven for around 20 minutes or until the fish is cooked through and has a nice color.

Top off the dish with shrimp and serve with rice, pasta, or potatoes and asparagus or broccoli.

OUR FAMILY'S PIZZA

Serves 4

This recipe makes two thin pizzas that fit on a baking pan each. The secret with a good pizza is to add the cheese directly after the tomato sauce as this keeps the base crispy. After that you can top it off with any goodies you like. You can garnish with some arugula just as the pizzas come out of the oven.

Pizza dough
0.9 ounce (25 g) yeast
1 cup (250 ml) lukewarm water
2 tablespoons oil
1 teaspoon salt
3–3½ cups (700–800 ml) flour
Olive oil for brushing

Tomato sauce
14 ounces (400 g) canned crushed tomatoes
2 tablespoons tomato puree
½ tablespoon dried oregano
½ teaspoon salt
1 pinch granulated sugar

Toppings
Grated cheese, shredded ham, finely sliced red onion, thinly sliced cherry tomatoes, and some dabs of cream cheese, arugula once the pizza is baked

Other suggestions for fillings
Mozzarella, taco beef, ham, pepperoncini, olives, fried chicken, bacon, kebab meat, beef sirloin, pork tenderloin

Pizza salad
1 small white cabbage
1 saucepan of boiling water
3 capfuls of white vinegar
½ cup (100 ml) canola oil
1½ teaspoons salt
Freshly ground black pepper

Start with the pizza salad (or make it while the dough rises). Use a cheese slice or mandoline to finely shred the cabbage or use a food processor. Place the shreds in a sieve and pour the boiling water over it. Then rinse with ice cold water until the cabbage has cooled down. Leave to drain and then place in a bowl. Mix vinegar, canola oil, salt, and pepper and add the dressing to the bowl mixing well. Add more vinegar or salt and pepper if you like.

Crumble the yeast for the pizza dough into a bowl and mix with some water. Add the rest of the ingredients. Add as much flour as you need so that the dough just lets go of the edges and becomes smooth. You can knead the dough with a machine or a whisk with a hook attachment for 5 minutes. Cover the bowl and leave to rise for 45 to 60 minutes. Meanwhile preheat the oven to 475°F (250°C) so it is hot once the pizzas are ready to bake.

Brush 2 baking pans with some olive oil. Halve the dough and roll each out so it covers 1 pan.

Mix all the ingredients for the tomato sauce in a saucepan. Bring to a boil and leave to simmer for 10 minutes. Add more sugar or oregano to taste.

Divide the tomato sauce over the pizza bases and then sprinkle over the cheese. Then add the rest of the toppings. Bake the pizza in the middle of the oven for around 10 to 15 minutes or until it reaches a nice color.

Serve immediately with some arugula on top together with the pizza salad.

SWEET THINGS

Do you love chocolate, berries, or nuts as a sweet ending to a good dinner? In that case you are guaranteed to find the recipe you want here!

Among other things I will serve up fun pavlovas with fresh berries and a dreamy chocolate pie that doesn't even need to be baked. The recipes don't need a lot of work and most of the ingredients are things you can find at home. Serving up something sweet that also looks good never hurts, and with these recipes it is simple too. Isn't something sweet just the thing after a meal?

KEY LIME PIE

Serves around 8

A fantastic sweet and tangy dessert that I fell in love with after visiting Key West in Florida. This is my version of this world-famous pie.

Base
7 ounces (200 g) digestive biscuits
9 tablespoons (125 g) melted butter

Filling
28 ounces (800 g) canned, sweetened condensed milk
¾–1 cup (200 ml) freshly squeezed lime juice
Zest from 1 lime
6 egg yolks

Top off with
Lightly whipped cream
Finely grated lime zest

Preheat the oven to 345°F (170°C). Crush the biscuits into fine crumbs, either by hand or in a food processor. Place the crumbs in a bowl and add the butter. Make a crumbly mixture.

Press the mixture evenly into a springform pan, around 10 inches in diameter. Blind-bake the pie crust in the middle of the oven for 10 minutes and then lower the heat to 300°F (150°C).

Mix condensed milk, lime juice, and zest in a bowl. Whisk together the egg yolks and mix them into the bowl. Mix until the batter is smooth but don't overmix, then pour into the springform pan.

Bake the pie in the middle of the oven for 15 to 20 minutes (it should not change color or begin to brown).

Leave the pie to cool down and then chill for at least 4 hours in the fridge, preferably overnight. Cover with the cream, sprinkle some lime zest on top, and serve.

MINI PAVOLVAS WITH FRESH BERRIES

Makes 6 mini pavlovas/portions

Sweet and fresh at the same time! It's a super simple dessert that is perfect for parties.

3 egg whites at room temperature
1¼ cups (300 ml) granulated sugar
1 teaspoon freshly squeezed lemon juice
1 tablespoon cornstarch
3½ ounces (100 g) melted dark chocolate

Top off with
Whipped cream
Fresh berries (strawberries, blueberries, red currants)
Sliced star fruit (optional)
Icing sugar (optional)
Lemon balm leaves

Preheat the oven to 300°F (150°C). Whisk the egg whites in a clean bowl to make a stiff foam. Add the sugar a little at a time and keep whisking until the meringue batter is firm and stiff. Fold in the lemon juice and then the cornstarch.

Pipe or dollop 6 meringue bottoms on a baking tray with parchment paper, around 4 to 5 inches in diameter. Bake the meringue for 20 minutes and then reduce the heat to 212°F (100°C) and bake for a further 40 minutes.

Leave the meringues to cool down and then drizzle the melted chocolate over them. Leave to completely cool.

Top each pavlova with some whipped cream, berries, and fruit.

Dust each pavlova with some icing sugar if you like and decorate with lemon balm leaves.

Serve immediately.

MILK CHOCOLATE TRUFFLE CAKE WITH CRUNCH

Serves 6–8

A clever chocolate pie that doesn't need baking.

Base
7 ounces (200 g) digestive biscuits
⅓ cup (75 g) melted butter

Filling
14 ounces (400 g) canned dulce de leche

Truffle spread
⅔ cup (150 ml) whipping cream
14 ounces (400 g) schweizernöt chocolate bars
  (chocolate with hazelnut)
2 pinches flaked salt

Topping
¾ cup (200 ml) whipping cream
Cocoa powder

To serve
About ½ pound fresh berries

Crush the biscuits into crumbs and mix with the melted butter. Press the mixture evenly into a springform pan, 9¾ inches in diameter. Leave to chill in the fridge for 20 minutes.

Spread the dulce de leche evenly over the base and leave to cool while you make the truffle spread.

Boil the cream in a saucepan. Remove from the heat and break the chocolate into the saucepan, letting it melt while stirring.

Spread the truffle evenly on top and sprinkle some flaked salt over it. Leave in the fridge for at least 4 hours.

Whip the cream and pipe it into peaks along the edge. Dust some cocoa on the peaks.

Serve with fresh berries.

BERRY CRUMBLE IN A GLASS

Makes 10 small portions

A dessert that you can prepare several hours in advance. Quick to make and easy to eat!

7 ounces (200 g) digestive biscuits
¼ cup + 3 tablespoons (100 g) melted salted butter
14 ounces (400 g) canned dulce de leche
About ½ pound (250 g) fresh berries such as
    raspberries and blueberries
1 cup (250 ml) whipping cream
3 roughly chopped large Heath bars
    (1.4 ounce/39 grams each)
Lemon balm leaves to garnish

Crush the biscuits into fine crumbs, either by hand or in a food processor. Place the crumbs in a bowl and add the butter. Make a crumbly mixture.

Layer the crumbs, dulce de leche, and berries in nice glasses. Lightly whisk the cream and place on top. Sprinkle over the crushed candy bars and garnish with some lemon balm before serving.

BANANA SPLIT

Serves 1

You are never too old for a banana split, ever. Make a mountain of these treats in a glass bowl. The amounts in this recipe serve 1 person, so you just need to multiply it—and it's better to make a little too much than too little, as it will get eaten!

1 banana, halved
¾ cup (200 ml) ice cream, preferably different flavors
¼ cup (50 ml) whipping cream
Cherries
Strawberries dipped in chocolate
Cookies, wafers, or meringue
Chocolate sauce
Sprinkles

Cover the bottom of the bowl with bananas and then layer ice cream and cream on top. Finish off with the cherries, strawberries, and cookies. Drizzle chocolate sauce over all the yummy stuff and finish off with some fun sprinkles.

PINEAPPLE PIE WITH RASPBERRIES

Serves around 6

A fresh and crispy dessert.

Pie dough
1¾ cups (400 ml) flour
1½ teaspoons baking powder
14 tablespoons (200 g) butter
½ cup (125 ml) granulated sugar

Filling
17½ ounces (500g) canned crushed pineapple
2 eggs
¾ cup (200 ml) crème fraiche
⅓ cup (100 ml) granulated sugar
1 teaspoon vanilla sugar
20 fresh raspberries

To garnish
Lemon balm leaves

To serve
Vanilla ice cream

Preheat the oven to 350°F (175°C). Mix flour and baking powder in a bowl. Cut the butter into cubes and add it to the bowl with the sugar. Quickly work into a dough and press it into 6 springform pans, around 3½ inches in diameter.

Drain the pineapple juice from the cans and mix together the pineapple pieces with the rest of the ingredients for the filling except the raspberries. Divide the filling between the springform pans and press the raspberries into the batter. Bake in the middle of the oven for around 40 minutes, or until the pie has some color.

Leave to cool down or chill before serving. You can garnish the pies with some lemon balm if you like and serve with a good vanilla ice cream.

PECAN PIE

Serves around 6

Anyone who tastes this pie will ask for the recipe!

Pie dough
4⅓ ounces (125 g) butter
1¼ cups (300 ml) flour
1 pinch salt
3 tablespoons cold water

Filling
9 tablespoons (125 g) butter
1¼ cups (300 ml) light corn syrup
⅔ cup (150 ml) light muscovado sugar
2 tablespoons flour
1 pinch salt
7 ounces (200 g) roughly chopped pecans
2 eggs, lightly whisked
1 teaspoon vanilla sugar

To serve
Lightly whipped cream
Vanilla ice cream
A few lemon balm leaves (optional)
Fresh raspberries (optional)

Preheat the oven to 350°F (175°C). Start with the dough for the pie: cut the butter into cubes and place in a bowl with the rest of the ingredients. Quickly work it into a dough and then press it into a pie pan, around 8½ to 9¾ inches in diameter (22 to 24 cm). Blind-bake the pie crust for 10 minutes. Meanwhile make the filling.

Mix butter, syrup, sugar, flour, and salt in a saucepan. Bring to a boil and then simmer while stirring for around 2 to 3 minutes. Remove the saucepan from the heat and add nuts, eggs, and vanilla sugar.

Pour the filling into the pie crust and bake for 35 to 40 minutes. If the pie starts to brown too quickly, cover it with aluminum foil. Leave the pie to cool down and then chill in the fridge.

Garnish the pie with some lemon balm and raspberries if desired.

Serve together with a good vanilla ice cream and some lightly whipped cream.

WEEKLY MENUS

Surely it's not just me who thinks that having a weekly menu is great! It gives you a good overview of the weekly meals and makes it easier to do a big grocery shop.

It can seem daunting at times to try to put together a menu when there are so many recipes to choose from and so many different tastes to cater to. This is why I have put together a menu for four weeks with my and my family's favorite recipes, which has been a savior more than once.

I always make sure I vary what I place on the dinner table, which is why each week contains a mix of recipes that makes sure you get fish, chicken, meat, and even something vegetarian at least once a week. In this way you get the best of everything!

Week 1

Day	Dinner
Monday	Potato pancakes with lingonberries (page 115)
Tuesday	Sausage soup (page 72)
Wednesday	Caesar salad with shrimp (page 90)
Thursday	Halloumi stroganoff (page 116)
Friday	Our family's fish burgers (page 96)
	Dessert: Pineapple pie with raspberries (page 153)
Saturday	Homemade chicken nuggets with basil sauce (page 50)
	Dessert: Milk chocolate truffle cake with crunch (page 147)
Sunday	Our family's pizza (page 138)

Week 2

Day	Dinner
Monday	Vegetable patties with halloumi (page 119)
Tuesday	Pasta with creamy salmon sauce (page 98)
Wednesday	Lasagna de luxe (page 68)
Thursday	Heavenly pork chops (page 29)
Friday	Tacos with hot shrimp and guacamole (page 85)
	Dessert: Banana split (page 150)
Saturday	Planked salmon (page 129)
	Dessert: Key lime pie (page 142)
Sunday	Chicken kebab with pita bread (page 46)

Week 3

Day	Dinner
Monday	Panko-fried cod with dill stewed potatoes (page 101)
Tuesday	Spaghetti with chicken and bacon sauce (page 38)
Wednesday	Thai red stew (page 120)
Thursday	Mozzarella filled meatballs with mashed potatoes (page 71)
Friday	Homemade fish sticks with cold dill sauce (page 82)
	Dessert: Mini pavlovas with fresh berries (page 145)
Saturday	Langos (with lots of accompaniments) (page 130)
	Dessert: Pecan pie (page 154)
Sunday	Souvlaki skewers with tzatziki and my Greek salad (page 22)

Week 4

Day	Dinner
Monday	Spicy salmon with couscous salad and crayfish mix (page 94)
Tuesday	Creole stew with chorizo (page 30)
Wednesday	Granddad's tasty lentil stew (page 107)
Thursday	Oven-baked Italian chicken (page 42)
Friday	Cod tacos with pickled red onions (page 93)
	Dessert: Berry crumble in a glass (page 149)
Saturday	Pulled pork with pickled red onions (page 135)
	Dessert: Banana split (page 150)
Sunday	Our family's pizza (page 138)

RECIPE INDEX

PORK, BEEF & VEAL

Bacon-wrapped pork tenderloin with potato and parsnip puree and red wine sauce	34
Creole stew with chorizo	30
Fancy pork tenderloin stew	17
Forest stew	32
Hearty stew with minute steak	21
Heavenly pork chops	29
Pork tenderloin in a creamy gorgonzola sauce	25
Souvlaki skewers with tzatziki and my Greek salad	22
Sweet and sour stew with chili and pepper	26
Wienerschnitzel	18

CHICKEN

Chicken gratin with smoked ham	49
Chicken in ajvar sauce	45
Chicken in green peppercorn sauce with duchess potatoes	53
Chicken kebab with pita bread	46
Chicken skewers with rice and peanut butter sauce	55
Flying Jacob	56
Homemade chicken nuggets with basil sauce	50
Jenny's Manor house chicken	41
Oven-baked Italian chicken	42
Spaghetti with chicken and bacon sauce	38

SAUSAGE & GROUND MEATS

Beef patties with feta and cream sauce	63
Fake pork tenderloin	77
Falu sausage gratin	78
Halloumi baked falu sausage	67
Hearty pork & beef soup	60
Lasagne de luxe	68
Loaded meatloaf	64
Mozzarella filled meatballs with mashed potatoes	71
Sausage soup	72
Taco pie	74

FISH & SEAFOOD

Caesar salad with shrimp	90
Cod tacos with pickled red onion	93
Fish stew with lemon aioli	89
Homemade fish sticks with cold dill sauce	82
Our family's fish burgers	96
Oven-baked lemon salmon	86
Panko-fried cod with dill stewed potato	101
Pasta with creamy salmon sauce	98
Spicy salmon with couscous salad and crayfish mix	94
Tacos with hot shrimp and guacamole	85

VEGETARIAN

Broccoli and blue cheese pie	111
Cabbage soup with root vegetables	108
Colorful wok with noodles	104
Granddad's tasty lentil stew	107
Halloumi stroganoff	116
Pasta with a creamy vegetable sauce	112
Pasta with homemade pesto	123
Potato pancakes with lingonberries	115
Thai red stew	120
Vegetable patties with halloumi	119

PARTIES & FESTIVITIES

Langos	130
Our family's pizza	138
Planked salmon	129
Pulled pork with pickled red onion	135
Roasted beef sirloin with luxurious hasselback potatoes and blue cheese sauce	126
Sandwich cake	132
The fish wives' luxurious fish gratin	136

SWEET THINGS

Banana split	150
Berry crumble in a glass	149
Key lime pie	142
Milk chocolate truffle cake with crunch	147
Mini pavlovas with fresh berries	145
Pecan pie	154
Pineapple pie with raspberries	153